AMAZON ECHO DOT

3rd Generation

Essential User Guide for Echo Dot and Alexa

2019 Updated

By

William Scott

TABLE OF CONTENTS

WANT TO STAY UPDATED WITH ECHO DOT?

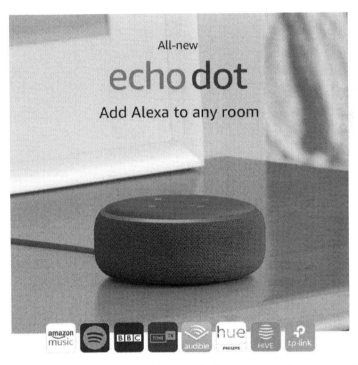

Before we begin, I would like to inform you about our **FREE UPDATES** for the latest in Amazon Echo Dot, Alexa and Smart Assistants.

The Amazon Echo Dot and other Alexa Enabled Devices are still in early stages of smart home evolution. In fact, you are one of the EARLY ADOPTORS of this technology. The smart assistant industry is changing so fast with new devices, apps and skills being released almost every other day that it is almost impossible to STAY FRESH.

That is where we come in. Staying in the know about new

developments in the Smart Assistive Industry is what we are here for. So if you want the LATEST news, tips and tricks we would highly recommend you to please sign up for our FREE newsletter. Do not worry, we hate spam as much as you do and your details will be safe with us.

You can find the link for Signup at the end of this book, in the Conclusion section.

WHY YOU NEED THIS BOOK

"Alexa, remind me to call Mom at 2 PM."

"Alexa, Wake me up at 6 am"

You wake up in the morning at 6 am with the sound of birds chirping. You get up and head straight to your kitchen where a freshly brewed cup of your favourite double espresso is waiting for you. While sipping coffee, Echo reads out your customised news flash and weather report. It is snowing outside, so you decide to head over to your treadmill instead of going out for a run. In the meantime, your soft-boiled eggs are ready and you have your breakfast while Echo reads out your calendar for the day. Next, you take a quick shower and then ask Echo to order a cab. The cab arrives and you head straight to office.

This is my morning routine, what makes this particular anecdote exceptional is that Amazon Echo Dot choreographed this without the touch of a button. All I did was make some routines and give it a few commands and my mornings are seamless.

The time for disposing off wires and switches has come. You enter the world of Alexa, the wonderful assistant that switches off the lights out when you go to sleep and sends you a message when she senses smoke in the house. Are you ready to be amazed how easier Echo Dot will make your life? Read on and find why the world is going one step smarter with the all new Amazon Echo Dot.

Welcome to your SMART LIFE!

Amazon Echo Dot 3rd Generation is a voice-activated smart speaker. It is compatible with an ever-increasing number of smart devices and online platforms. It can answer basic queries, control smart devices, stream music from any of your cloud accounts, receive and make call and much more. It responds to the wake word "Alexa".

Alexa is a cloud-based, voice-activated personal assistant. She has an incredible variety of skills and can be pre-programmed to carry out errands. As you start to use the all new Echo Dot, Alexa adapts to your speech patterns, vocabulary, and personal preferences. And you can also download and install third party Alexa Skills on your Echo device to enhance its capabilities!

This book is written for those who are puzzled by the Amazon Echo Dot and other Alexa Enabled devices, just like I was when I bought the 1st generation Amazon Echo. This book is written from my personal experience and anecdotal evidence from early Echo Users who have helped me adapt this smart device into my life in the last three years. I am using Amazon Echo and Alexa since the 1st generation Amazon Echo was released back in 2014. And I published my first Amazon Echo user manual in 2016.

If you are a tech savvy person, the kind of user that LOVES to figure it out new devices themselves no matter what or is happy to spend a few hours on Google looking for answers then probably you don't need this book. We are very honest in admitting that you can probably find a lot if the information in this book by looking for it on Amazon Help, Google or tinkering with your Echo device just like I did. That is, if you are willing to spend the time and effort to find that information.

However, if you were surprised or disappointed to find how little information comes in the box with your Amazon Echo Dot and prefer to have at hand, like so many users, a comprehensive, straightforward, step by step Amazon Echo Dot guide, to finding your way around your new device, then this book is definitely for you.

This book will help you save a lot of time and effort of going out and finding all that information to make the best use of your new Amazon Echo Dot. And, you will also get regular updated about Alexa, Echo Devices and Smart Home Assistants once you SIGNUP for our weekly new letter. That way, you will be able to find all the information you are looking for without beating you head around. If we have missed anything specific you were looking for in this book or elsewhere about Alexa/Echo Devices/Smart Home Assistants we would be pleased to help you. Do write to us, our email address is in the conclusion.

Through this book, our goal is to help you setup Echo Dot and start using it like a pro in no time.

- Connect all your smart devices at home and use Echo Dot as your hub to control them.

- Setup routines like making coffee, reading your calendar and switching off lights at night.

- Shop on Amazon, order pizza and get Alexa to entertain your kids.

Alexa combines with countless smart devices and apps to help you automate your daily life. So, let's begin the journey to discover how to use your Amazon Echo to its best advantage.

Learn more, turn up the thermostat, open the shades and put on your favorite music...hmm "Alexa, turn the thermostat up..."

SECTION #1

HOW TO SETUP YOUR
ECHO DOT

INTRODUCTION

"*Alexa, set a timer for 15 minutes.*"

Welcome! Thank you for buying this book. We are excited to have you On-board this journey to the world of Amazon Echo Dot and Alexa. Before we begin let me remind you to Sign up for our Alexa Newsletter so that you remain updated with all the latest developments with Amazon Echo. The Signup information is available at the end if this book in the Conclusion.

How To Use This Book

To get a clear understanding, I would advise you to read the book cover to cover. So that you know how this book is structured. Then you can go back to particular sections and refer to a topics individually. We have purposely kept this book to the point so that you can consume it in an hour and get straight on with enjoying your Amazon Echo.

In a nutshell Amazon Echo Dot is a voice-activated speaker from

Amazon that

- Acts as your smart personal assistant
- Performs digital errands at your command
- Controls smart devices

Much More Than a Speaker

Many simply assume that the Amazon Echo Dot is a regular speaker. However, calling Echo Dot a speaker is far from accurate. It definitely does function as an excellent speaker, but it is primarily a personal assistant that can help you with

- Running your daily chores and errands at Home and Office
- Freeing up you time by carrying out repetitive tasks
- Calling or messaging anyone with a supported Echo device or the Alexa App on their phone for FREE.
- Controlling your smart devices – Lights, Thermostat, Crockpot etc.
- Informing you about News, Sports Updates, Weather, Traffic and more
- Playing your favorite music at a voice command

And much more....

The Echo Dot has been designed to respond to voice commands. It will reply if you call its "Wake Word". You can choose from among four of the following wake words.

- Alexa
- Echo
- Amazon
- Computer

When you want your Echo Dot to do something, then you will have to start out by saying the Wake Word. The device will acknowledge the same and you don't even need a remote or your phone for turning it on. This does sound good, doesn't it?

The Amazon Echo Dot brings a new dimension of supplementary ease to a smart home. Users can control settings of interconnected devices through a simple voice command. By doing away with dials, switches, and buttons, Echo helps multiple users with different accents activate or change settings on digital devices from far away. It is especially useful for people with disability.

You can 'command' your Echo Dot with voice messages that last for 2 minutes at a time. You would know soon how amazing it feels to have an assistant that does exactly as told and gets smarter with every interaction.

CHAPTER 1
Features That Make Echo Dot Amazing

Technical details

- Weight: 300 grams
- Price: $49.99
- Size: 99 x 99 x 43 mm
- Colors: Charcoal, Heather Gray & Sandstone
- Audio: Built-in speaker, 3.5 mm stereo output
- Connectivity: Dual-band Wi-Fi 802.11/a/b/g/n/ac, Bluetooth connectivity
- Power: Power adapter 15W, DC power

Ease of use

The new Echo Dot is easier to use than never before. In fact, it is easier than using a cell phone. You don't have to worry about inserting a SIM card, installing apps, registering your name -simply turn the device on and start using it.

Even if you have never before used a personal assistant service, it doesn't take more than a few hours to get a hang of it. The step-by-step instructions in this book will help you in getting started. Using an Echo Dot is pretty easy. You will simply have to plug it in, follow the simple instructions, and that's about it.

Built

The 3rd generation Echo Dot is aesthetically pleasing, and its futuristic appearance will easily blend in with your home décor.

For the new Echo Dot Amazon has done away with the shiny plastic exterior and replaced it with a softer, more attractive design. The puck-shaped device is now encased with a fabric design, a rounded top with no sharp edges. The fact that it no longer has an Amazon logo on makes it feels like a more premium product than its predecessors. The exterior is similar to its close competitor the Google Home Mini and is available in three new colors: Charcoal, Heather Grey, and Sandstone. One does wish Amazon had not played it so conservative and come with brighter color options.

The all new Echo Dot 3rd generation is **bigger** and **heavier** with a better anti-slide silicone grip at the base to prevent skidding. The speaker top has four control buttons and four pin sized microphones to help hear your voice better over the significantly large volume.

This time around Amazon has ditched the micro- USB port and used a small cylindrical DC power tip instead with a rounded wall plug.

Sound

The third gen echo is a much better speaker unlike its predecessors, and sound quality is great. Under the encased fabric is a single 1.6 inch speaker that fires 360 degrees. This is a big jump from the prior models (1.1inch speaker). The new Echo with a bigger driver can deliver a more balanced, robust sound with lower distortions even at higher volumes. Amazon claims that the 3rd-gen is 70% louder than its 2nd gen counterpart.

There is definitely more bass and it no longer feels like you are listening to music on the external speaker of a cheap phone. If, however you need to connect to an external speaker, the Dot has a 3.5-millimeter port. You can also connect to an external speaker wirelessly via Bluetooth.

Another cool feature worth mentioning is that the new Echo Dot supports stereo pairing. This means that you can now pair any two Echo speakers as dedicated right and left channels or pair them with the Echo Sub for a boasted bass. For details on how to do this, please refer to the Chapter 9.

Voice recognition

Echo Dot is your personal assistant at home that you can share with friends and family. To make sure that user experience is unique for each individual even when sharing a single device, Amazon has added voice recognition as a Alexa skill. This means that you can train Alexa to recognise individual voices and get personalised information.

FAR-FIELD
VOICE RECOGNITION

You need to create a voice profile for each user and when you do that Alexa recognises each user by their name and gives personalized answers and play music as per user preference.

Lighting

The way the Echo Dot changes colors, tells you what's happening with the device. When the Echo Dot is connected but has not been activated using the wake-up command the ring will show no color. When she wakes up the light turns SOLID BLUE with a small section of cyan. When she tries to process your request, the light is SOLID BLUE with a spinning cyan ring. When it turns ORANGE, this means that the device is connecting to the Internet or the WIFI network. The light will turn a darker shade of orange if it connects to the network and if not, it will turn VOILET. When you are changing the volume of the Echo, it will show a white ring. This ring turns RED when you mute the Dot. Pulsing GREEN light means you are receiving a call while YELLOW ring means you have a notification or message waiting for you.

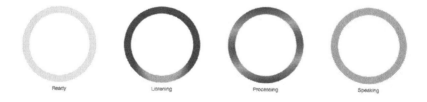

| Ready | Listening | Processing | Speaking |

Privacy

This seems to be a huge concern for a lot of people who make use of personal assistant devices like the Echo Dot. The Dot is designed to pick up every word that it hears and it makes use of its cloud processing system. In such a case, how will you make sure that your personal information isn't being divulged?

You needn't worry about this at all. When you are discussing any private matters, you can just mute the device by pressing the MUTE button on top of the Echo Dot. Press this switch, and the Dot will stop collecting any information.

CHAPTER 2
Setup Your Echo Dot

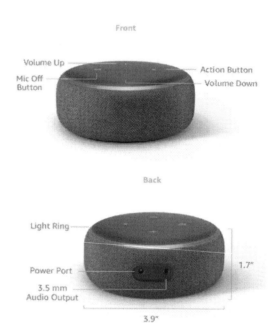

What's in the Box

- Echo dot
- Power Adapter 15W
- Quick Start Guide

What you Need to Buy

A 3.5mm output jack to connect your Echo Dot to external speakers.

Once you open the box, you will see the main unit. Echo Dot is a small disc shaped device. It has got voice sensors, speakers and lights.

The shape helps in minimizing the space it requires. However, it is more effective if there's a little room around the device for better reception. The light ring on top of the Echo Dot turns blue when the device is switched on.

It is powered with the help of a plug-in adapter. You can put it on a metallic surface or even stick it against your cabinet depending on your convenience.

Don't let the small size of the Echo Dot fool you, it is extremely useful and worth the price. Its size allows you to place it anywhere and it is powerful enough to pick up on sounds, making it effective.

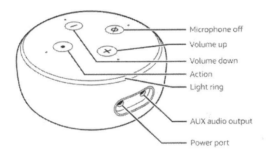

Step Setup Instructions

Step #1: Install Echo Dot in a Safe Place

For optimal performance only use the items included in your Echo Dot package. Try to find a place at least 10 inches from the walls, windows or any obstructions.

- Connect the power cable to your Echo Dot. It is worth noting that the 3rd generation no longer has a USB cable option unlike its predecessors.
- The LED light ring on top of your Echo will turn blue and will begin to spin. In a minute, the color will change to Orange and Alexa will greet you.

Step #2: Setup Echo Dot using Alexa App

Downloading the Alexa App

Go to the store on your mobile or computer. This could be Google Play Store, Apple App Store or Amazon Appstore. You can also choose to you can type *alexa.amazon.com* instead in your browser search bar. Search and download the *Alexa app* for Fire OS, Android or iOS. Sign into your account and follow the instructions in the app/website to complete the setup.

(Please note that Alexa app is not supported on Kindle Fire 1st or 2nd Generations)

Connect Your Echo to Wifi

Be sure to connect dual-band Wi-Fi networks and not use mobile hotspots. Echo Dot will not work when you use ad-hoc networks that are connected peer-to-peer.

- Open the Alexa app and go to **Settings**.
- Select your device and click on **Update Wi-Fi**.
- For first time users, click on **Select a new device**.
- Now, press the *Action* button on the Echo device.
- The light will turn orange and you will see a list of networks appear on your mobile device. Select your Wi-Fi network

18

and type the password if required.

- For cases where your network is not visible, scroll down the list and select **Add a Network**.
- If this does not work, click on **Rescan**.
- Now click **Connect** and Alexa is ready for use.

Step #3: Talk to Your Amazon Echo Dot for the First Time

To begin, we use the wake word – *Alexa. 'Alexa, play me some music'*. Or *'Alexa, what is the weather like today?'* When your voice reaches Echo Dot, the circular, blue LED lights on top of Echo Dot lights up – she is listening, and once your command is processed, Alexa will reply.

Alexa is always listening and waiting for her 'wake' word, so you do not have to raise your voice and can call her over the din of conversation or music. If many people ask her questions, Alexa picks out the individual accents of the people and separates the questions with ease. Then, you get the answers. *"Music playing"* and *"The weather is sunny with day temperatures of 90 degrees."*

Now that Alexa is responding to your commands let's move on the last step.

Step #4: Connect to Your Home Stereo System or Bluetooth Speaker

If required, you can connect your Echo Dot to external speakers using a 3.5mm jack cable. Or if you have a Bluetooth Speaker, you can to pair it with your speaker.

Pairing with Bluetooth Speaker

Please ensure that your Bluetooth speaker is places at least 3 feet from your Echo Dot for optimal performance.

- Put your speaker in pairing mode
- In your Alexa App Tap Menu and then Tap Settings

- Tap Echo Dot in your list of Alexa Devices
- Tap Bluetooth
- Tap You speaker when it appears in your list of Bluetooth devices

You're Done! Now you can start using your Echo Dot.

Now, wherever this paired speaker is ON, your Echo Dot will route all your audio through it.

If you decide to remove this speaker from your list of Bluetooth devices, just go back to Bluetooth in the settings and tap on the speaker and then tap on Forget Speaker.

Installing Echo Dot in Every Room

MADE FOR

ANY ROOM

The installation and setup procedure for multiple devices is the same as installing a single Echo Dot. With the new ESP technology, now there is no confusion when you address Alexa. The device nearest responds and carries out the command. The advantage of having an Echo Dot in every room means that you are using the full functionality of Alexa from anywhere in your house without the need of talking out loud or going back and forth.

CHAPTER 3
Voice Training Your Echo Dot

Now that the setup is complete its time for fun!

Say hello to your new Personal Assistant. In this chapter we will learn about all the errands you can get your new Echo Dot to run for you and start simplifying your life immediately. With the help of a voice command you will get the latest in sports, weather and traffic and news, order a cab or listen to your favorite Audiobook. But first let's train Echo Dot to recognize and understand our Voice.

Voice Training

In the first few weeks, you will have to be patient with Echo Dot. It's important to train your Echo Dot so that you can make the best use of this device without getting frustrated. Voice training is a fairly simple process but you need to be consistent with it for the first few days to get the best results.

It's best to get all members of your family to take turns speaking to Echo Dot. Before we start commanding our new Voice Assistant, we need to introduce everyone in the house to Echo Dot. So, line up everyone who would be using the Echo Dot and make them speak to it, one after the other. This is a really important step of the setup process and is referred to as VOICE TRAINING.

Doing this will help your Echo Dot respond accordingly and it does get better with practice. Eventually, it will be able to identify different users through their voice and use their name while responding back to them.

Each user should go through voice training multiple times. It will also help the users get accustomed to the way Echo Dot responds to your queries.

For starting a voice training session, you will have to open the Alexa app. Then go to the navigation panel on the home page and pick the Voice Training option. Press the Start button.

The next step is for you to say a phrase for the Echo Dot to listen to and comprehend. Try to include complex words to ensure that the Echo Dot can understand them. When you finish a phrase, choose the Next option at the bottom of the app screen to move on to the next one.

Speak in your natural voice, even if you have a heavy accent. You don't have to be too close to the device; it should be able to accept commands from any part of the room.

Once you're done speaking, you should introduce the next member of your family to the Echo Dot. They can then do the same as you just did – speak phrases so that the Echo Dot can listen to them and train it.

Each of you should speak about 25 phrases, trying to incorporate as many words as possible. The more the Echo Dot hears, the more it understands.

You can press the Pause button at any time, and if you think you've made a mistake then you can pick the Cancel option. Then press Repeat to try again.

Once everyone is done and you have recorded all the phrases, you can press the End Session button.

Your Echo Dot will now be able to understand you better. It should take most commands with ease and will rarely get confused. However, you can't expect it to be perfect from the beginning. The Echo's voice recognition is very good, but it will make the occasional mistake.

Once the Echo Dot is familiar with everyone, it will remember the preferences of every individual. The way it responds would be more relevant and it can make suggestions based on the user activity. For instance, if someone in your household keeps asking for news updates, then the next time that user calls out to the Echo Dot; it will start reading out the news updates automatically.

Learning is an ongoing process with the Amazon Echo Dot. It will learn new things constantly and better itself with time. You will be pleasantly surprised at the amount of improvement the Echo Dot demonstrates over several months as it trains itself to suit your needs.

Please remember, Echo Dot can identify up to a maximum of 20 voices, as long as they aren't similar. And, Echo Dot will NOT respond to someone whose voice it doesn't recognize. It will not take any commands from a stranger even if they turn her off and then switch her on again. A user needs to be introduced to Echo Dot before it can recognize a new voice.

CHAPTER 4
Alexa Commands

You can make these commands work on all Alexa enabled devices. Just use the following commands.

- *"Alexa, Stop"*
- *"Alexa, Volume [number Zero to Ten]"*
- *"Alexa, Unmute"*
- *"Alexa, Mute"*
- *"Alexa, Repeat"*
- *"Alexa, Cancel"*
- *"Alexa, Louder"*
- *"Alexa, Volume Up"*
- *"Alexa, Volume Down"*
- *"Alexa, Turn Down"*
- *"Alexa, Turn Up"*
- *"Alexa, Help"*

How to Get Help from Alexa

When you've got a question about your Echo Dot, you can simply ask Alexa about it.

To get some help from Alexa, just say the *Alexa* word followed by the following questions:

- *"What can you do?"*
- *"What are your new features?"*
- *"What do you know?"*
- *"Can you do math?"*
- *"How can/do I play music?"*
- *"How can/do I add music?"*
- *"What is Prime Music?"*
- *"What is Audible?"*
- *"What is Connected Home?"*
- *"What is Voice Cast?"*
- *"How can/do I pair to Bluetooth?"*
- *"How can/do I connect my calendar?"*
- *"What is an Alexa skill?"*
- *"How can/do I use skills?"*
- *"How can/do I set an alarm?"*

How to Ask Alexa for Basic Calculations

If you manage accounts or have to deal with figures, having a voice-activated calculator is quite helpful. The Echo can help you with simple calculations and even the more complicated ones. You can get it to perform such functions without having to touch the keypad.

- *"Alexa, one thousand eight hundred seventy-six (1,876) divided by four"*
- *"Alexa, three point four eight six (3.486) times twenty-four"*
- *"Alexa, convert 12 feet to centimeters"*
- *"Alexa, convert 7 tablespoons to milliliters"*
- *"Alexa, convert 35 Fahrenheit to Celsius"*

- *"Alexa, how many miles are in thirty kilometers?"*

How to Ask Alexa for Cooking Conversions

- *"Alexa, how many teaspoons in two tablespoon?"*
- *"Alexa, how many tablespoons in eighteen teaspoons?"*
- *"Alexa, how many pints in four gallons?"*
- *"Alexa, how many cups in four quarts?"*

Getting Information from Echo Dot

The next thing would be to customize your Echo Dot. You should add your LOCATION. This enables Echo Dot to serve you better. If it isn't able to identify your location, then you can enter your zip code and try. You can also select the date format and the option of using metric system is up to you as well. Cloud computing will be set up automatically and you don't have to do anything else. The last step would be to select a Wake Name. Alexa is the default name. However, you can choose Echo, Amazon or Computer as well.

Let me add here that limited choice of Wake Words is a big issue with consumers who want a more personalized device. Amazon is working to rectify this issue. But as of now we just have to work with these 4 wake words until they allow us to use our own customized wake words.

How to get Localized Information

- Go to Settings in the Alexa App
- Tap on Echo Dot Device Location
- Enter your Address with Zip Code
- Tap Save Changes

This will get you weather reports, local news and even pre-recorded shows relative to your area.

Ask Echo Dot for Latest Weather Report

To get the latest weather reports from your area use the following commands:

- *"Alexa, what's the weather?"*
- *"Alexa, will it rain tomorrow?"*
- *"Alexa, what's the weather in Los Angeles this weekend?"*
- *"Alexa, what's the weather in Dallas?"*
- *"Alexa, what will the weather be like in Boston tomorrow?"*
- *"Alexa, what's the weather in Silver City, New Mexico?"*
- *"Alexa, what's the extended forecast for Chicago?"*
- *"Alexa, what will the weather be like in San Diego on Thursday?"*
- *"Alexa, is it going to snow on Monday?"*

Setup Alarms and Timers on Your Echo Dot

For Alarms use the following commands

- *"Wake me up at [time]."*
- *"Set an alarm for [time]."*
- *"Set an alarm for [amount of time] from now."*

For Countdown Timers use the following commands

- *"Set a timer for [amount of time]."*
- *"Set the timer for [time]."*

For a comprehensive list of all the alarm and timer commands and the change the alarm sound volume please refer to the Amazon Help.

Ask Echo Dot for the Latest Flash Briefings

How to Hear Flash Briefings

You don't need a newspaper to keep up with current events anymore – and with the Echo Dot, you don't even have to look at a monitor or tablet. All you have to do is ask it for your flash briefing and it will read out all the news bulletins for you. It will give you at least the headlines, and might also read a snippet of the accompanying articles.

To hear flash briefings of the latest new updates, you can configure your Alexa App to include news from various sources: BBC, Economist, TMZ, and NPR etc. To hear the news, just say *"Alexa, what's my Flash Briefing?"* and Echo Dot will play the news from your selected sources.

Configuring Flash Briefings

- Open the Alexa app
- Tap the left navigation panel,
- Go to Settings
- Select **Flash Briefing**
- Customize your Flash Briefing: Shows, News Headlines, Weather Updates etc.

Ask Echo Dot for Real-time Traffic Updates

Traffic is a big headache for most commuters, but the Echo Dot can now help you beat it. You have to use the Alexa app to add in your origin and destination points, but after that, you can just ask the Echo Dot what traffic looks like between them. It will let you know the shortest route, as well as the best route in terms of current traffic conditions.

How to Configure the Traffic Information

To get the most efficient routes from your Echo Dot

- Go to settings on your Alexa App
- Tap on Change Address
- Input the address in the FROM and TO fields
- Tap Save Changes

This will get you the most accurate traffic information for your desired route

Get the Latest Sports Scores

The Echo Dot can also give you sports news, of course, but it goes one better than that by providing live scores as well. Gone are the days of repeatedly clicking the refresh button on a web page to keep track of a game. It currently works with the NBA, NFL, NHL, WNBA, MLB and a few other major leagues. Tennis and mixed martial arts haven't been added to this list as of now.

Just ask

- *"Alexa, what the score (team name) game?"*
- *"Alexa, when does (team name) play?"*

Order UBER with a Voice Command

- Open the Alexa App and tap the three-bar menu on Top Left Corner
- Tap Skills
- Under Skills, search for Uber
- Enable the Uber Skill
- Sign In to your Uber Account and tap Allow

For office-goers who use Uber often, pulling out the phone to call up Uber may become tedious. So, commanding Alexa seems to be more attractive. *"Alexa, Ask Uber for a ride."* And Alexa comes back with, *"Your Uber ride is on its way."* You understand the charm Echo has. One likes to talk to Alexa rather than a cab driver or manager anytime!

Get Echo Dot to Read Your Kindle Books

- *"Alexa, Read my Kindle book"*
- *"Alexa, Read my book <title>"*
- *"Alexa, Play the Kindle book <title>"*
- *"Alexa, Read < title>"*

Listen to Your Audio Books

- *"Alexa, Read <title>"*
- *"Alexa, Play the book <title>"*
- *"Alexa, Play the audiobook <title>"*
- *"Alexa, Play <title> from Audible"*

Get Echo Dot to Read Your Calendar

How to Connect your Google Calendar to Alexa

You can pair your Google Calendar with your Echo Dot, which makes it easy to keep your whole schedule in one place and access it whenever you need to. You'll be more efficient at home and in the office, and you'll never have to miss another deadline or event. You can activate this feature by going to Settings in the Alexa app.

Though you can use any calendar you like, the Google Calendar will help you take the first step.

To connect follow these simple steps:

- Open the Alexa App in your mobile
- Click on *Settings > Calendar > Link Google Calendar Account*

You log in with your Google account and when you activate Alexa, you can check your schedule though you cannot write in new events. For that, you need to integrate the IFTTT recipe.

There are other recipes as well that can come handy, such as Add your To Do list to Google Calendar or Add a Sports Game to your Google Calendar. To check the complete list please visit IFTTT.COM

Do this on your calendar

"Alexa, what's on my calendar?" or *"Alexa, when is my next event?"* will give you the answers, *"You have a golf game with Martin at 3:00 PM today"* and *"Your next event is at 11:00 AM – A*

get together with your stockholders."

When naming your tasks, you must take care to see you avoid the use of the first person. *"I'm home"* or *"I want the news"* will not be as Alexa-friendly as *"Arrive Home"* and *"News Update."*

Add a household member to your Amazon Echo Dot

You can add multiple household members to your Echo Dot. You can share digital content with other members and also collaborate with them on the to-do lists, calendars etc.

- Open the Alexa app
- Go to Settings
- Go to Household Profile
- Sign in to your account.
- Click Continue.
- Enter the amazon account information for the person you want to add.
- Click Join Household.

If you want to check which member profile is active use the following commands

- "Alexa, which account is this?"
- "Alexa, which profile am I using?"

Please remember that once other members are on Echo Dot they will be able to shop from your account as well. For an additional

Remove a household member from Amazon Echo Dot

- Go to Settings.
- Go to In an Amazon household with [user name] and tap
- Tap Remove User

CHAPTER 5
Using Alexa Skills on your Echo Dot

Create custom greeting cards for birthdays, anniversaries, and more.

"Alexa, help me create a greeting card."

Get started ·

Alexa SKILL Commands

Your Amazon Echo comes with a set of built in abilities. To enhance these abilities or to add new abilities to your Echo Dot add new Alexa Skills that are developed by Amazon or third-party Skills developers. You can find these Skills on your Alexa App.

These skills are the Alexa equivalent of iOS/Android Apps for your Smart Phone. Alexa Skills development platform is developing fast.

All skills support Launch command and Stop command and majority support the Help command.

Launch

Just say....

- "Alexa, launch [skill name]"

The skill will be launched and you will come to know that hearing the welcome message for the particular skill. Some information about the skill and applicable sample commands will be included in the message.

Stop

This one is straightforward. One quick hack: you can actually say *"Alexa, Stop"* even when Echo is speaking. Just be loud enough so that Alexa is able to hear you out over her voice.

Help

Most of the Alexa Skills have a help function except some Skills, which are pretty straightforward. To access this help, just say, "Help," and Alexa will read out the particular Skill's Help file to you.

Game Skills

- **Jeopardy!**

So, you want to get the same experience as the contestants on the show? So you know that every Jeopardy! category now has an "extra" 6th clue and that you can play those clues on Alexa! Test your knowledge every weekday with a single voice command and play the same categories you saw on the latest episode! Choose from sports, pop culture , world history , travel .

- **Escape the Room**

You need to search your room , pick up items and solve puzzles which will help you escape from the room . There are three rooms in the game based on the level of difficulty and you can choose which one to play .You can ask for hints which will help you make the escape in case you get stuck .You can track also track your statistics and how fast you escape from each room.

- **Would You Rather for Family**

This is a simple though addictive game where you have to choose between two silly situations and you can choose one of them. The questions are fun and engaging and there is no right answer, just lots of fun and laughter! You can play this with friends and family at a party or sleepover or family game night . Alone and want to kill time – you can also play it by yourself.

- **Song Quiz**

Listen to thousands of songs by your favorite artists from the past 60 years. Guess the correct title and artist for points. Challenge your friends and family in live competitions or compete head to head against music fans across the country! Master playlists from each decade.

- **True or False?**

Think you're a trivia pro? This is a fun game to test your knowledge about the world by answering either "true" or "false". The rules are simple, but the questions aren't.

- **Assassin's Creed® Odyssey Spartan**

The official skill of Assassin's Creed Odyssey, Alexios is designed to be the ultimate tool for life at home and in the game world. With answers to over 500 questions, Alexios is similar to other smart assistants, but has a more Spartan-like attitude. Just open the skill by saying "Alexa, open The Spartan" and then ask any questions that you might ask your usual Alexa-enabled device (e.g. "Alexa, ask The Spartan What's the weather like?" Alexa, ask The Spartan to set an alarm.", "Alexa, ask The Spartan to tell me a joke.").

Productivity Skills

- **Sleep and Relaxation Sounds**

Sleep Sounds lets you play ambient sounds to help you sleep peacefully or block out unwanted noise at work or home. With over 125 high quality sounds to choose from, you'll be able to sleep better, stay focused, study without interruption, relax quickly, meditate more effectively, and get your baby to go to sleep faster! If there's a sound you'd like to see added, just e-mail us at support@sleepsounds.io.

- **Find My Phone**

Find My Phone allows you to easily call your lost phone from Alexa! Now supports adding other numbers! Say "Alexa, Find My Phone" to call your phone at any time. To add a family member, say: "Alexa, ask find my phone to add another number", then say "Alexa, ask Find My Phone to call <name>" If you enjoy the skill, please do leave us a 5 star review as it helps other people find it and enjoy it too! :)

- **Sleep Sounds: Ocean Sounds**

Ocean Sounds helps you sleep peacefully or block out unwanted noise at work or home. You'll be able to sleep better, stay focused, study without interruption, relax quickly, meditate more effectively, and get your baby to go to sleep faster!

CHAPTER 6
Alexa Routines

An Alexa Routine allows you to control your smart home using single commands. It is not limited to just turning a device on or off but how these devices will act on your command. For example, changing the color or dimming some light, setting up your room temperature for the night.

Alexa is now capable of executing location-based routines that are executed when you either leave or arrive at a place (e.g. Home or work). It is also possible to add temperature and motion-based routines that are triggered when motion is detected, or the temperature is not in the desired temperature range. Another great use of Alexa routine is to be able to create a time limited music routine which is ideal for white noise.

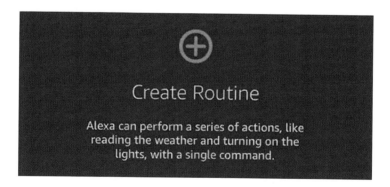

Start an Alexa routine

To start an Alexa Routine, simply head to the Alexa app and go to the menu where you will see a list of your current routines and Amazon suggested routines. You can either tap one of these routines or select the + **icon** the top-right corner to create a routine from scratch.

On the screen simply follow the instructions. Select **When this happens** which is the short command you would give to Alexa. You can choose how the routine will be triggered – whether by an Alexa command or using a timed routine, when choosing a command to trigger the routine, just type it in the app.

Now it's time to **Add action.** Press the + next to Add action button and choose which action you want triggered for your routine. Keep in mind that you do not need to build these from scratch. If you have specific Groups or Scenes set up already, you can use them.

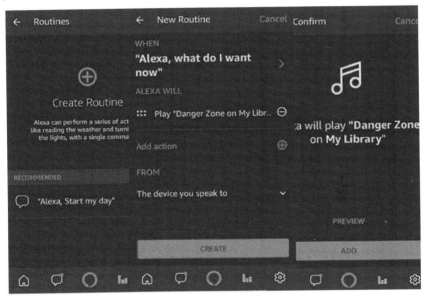

To modify or delete a Routine, open the Alexa app, go to the Routines section and choose the routine you want to edit or delete under the Enabled section.

CHAPTER 7
Alexa Blueprints

Alexa Blueprints is a way for you to create your own custom skills for your Alexa devices, without having the need to learn how to code. With the new sharing feature now, you can make a custom-made skill for a friend or family. You can create your own trivia games, write adventure stories, create custom answers for specific questions and much more.

To begin, head to Blueprints home page and login to your Amazon account. Now you can begin creating your custom skill.

Below are a few Blueprints

Chore Chart- Schedule and Track Weekly Chores.

Family Trivia- A family game, brush up on your family history.

Family Jokes- Create a list of your favorite family jokes.

Flashcards- Study, Test yourself and Master any subject.

Babysitter- Lets your baby sitter easily find things, remember steps, and get important information regarding your baby.

Personal Trainer- Plan your workout routines and schedule.

Sci-Fi- Great for a group, lets you create an interactive story.

CHAPTER 8
New Alexa Features for your Echo Dot

Amazon has introduced an array of new Alexa features for 2019 that will help in making your life more entertaining, convenient and safe. The new features are targeted for improving your daily productivity, better smart home monitoring, enhancing your entertainment experience with your family and friends.

Making Your Home Smarter and Safer with Alexa

Alexa Guard

Alexa Guard can help listen for certain specific sounds like smoke alarm going off, carbon monoxide alarm detector sound, high pitched squeal of a security alarm or that of glass breaking while you are away. Simple say "Alexa, I'm leaving" to activate Guard. Alexa can then send you notifications to your smart phone when it hears something suspiciously close to any of those sounds. It can also integrate to your security system from Ring or ADT and send notifications straight to the dispatchers monitoring your home.

Alexa is also capable of using Away Lighting to intuitively turn lights on and off when supported by a smart lighting system to help deter intruders.

Alexa Hunches

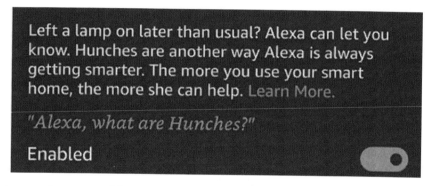

As you interact with your smart home, Alexa learns more about your daily activities and routines. Based on this it creates a digital profile of your daily routines. The AI inbuilt in Alexa attempts to replicate human hunches to produce guesses and predict your future needs. If it notices anything is different or amiss from your normal routine it uses deep neural network to find out why you would have done something differently. If at night you switch off the living room lights and the lights are still on when you say "Alexa, good night," she will prompt you by saying "By the way, your living room light is on. Do you want me to turn it off?"

WIFI Simple Setup

Amazon wants to make the process of setting up your smart home a breeze. Wi-Fi Simple setup is part of Amazon's larger initiative – frustration free set up which also includes ZigBee set up. Alexa will share your Wi-Fi credentials with compatible smart home devices so that connecting devices will become as simple as just plugging them in. Amazon has promised to keep the information encrypted so that you can easily connect to smart devices without compromising on your home security.

To begin with this option will be available with new Echo devices, the new Amazon Smart Plug, and Amazon Basics Microwave.

Making Your Life More Convenient with Alexa

Location based Routines

Alexa Routines now lets you customize your daily routine more than ever before by adding location-based Alexa Routines that can trigger when you leave or arrive at work or home. It also lets you add timed delays in between Alexa Routine actions; add time-limited music which is great for white noise ; and Alexa Routines that get activated when the temperature in a room is not in the optimal temperature range, or when a motion is detected.

Location-Based Reminders

"Alexa, remind me to call Monica when I leave office," and she will diligently remind you of things to do or errands to run when you leave or arrive at home or work. When you arrive, she will speak the reminder and send a text notification to your smart phone.

Cook with Alexa

Echo is now more useful in the kitchen than ever before. Just ask Alexa for step by step cooking instructions from Side Chef, The Kitchn, Allrecipies, Epicurious or Food52. Say "Alexa, let's start cooking," and she will guide you through your favorite recipe step by step.

Multi-step Requests

Alexa can now handle a multi-step request. If you need to add a few things to your shopping list, just say "Alexa, add cat food, paper towel and bananas to my shopping list." or if you want to play a song at a certain volume, just say "Alexa, play Pandora at volume 7."

Email Integration

If you have a Hotmail, Gmail or Outlook account you will now be able to ask Alexa if you have received any emails from a certain person. All you need to do is link your email account in your Alexa app and say, "Alexa, do I have emails from Kevin?"

Even More Calling Options

With your new Echo Dot you can connect with any Skype user from around the world. All you need to say is, "Alexa, call John Skype" and she will connect with the user John on Skype assuming you know John.

Whisper Mode

Now you don't have to worry about waking up your baby seeping in the next room or your spouse sleeping next to you while commanding Alexa. The new Whisper mode lets you whisper commands to Alexa, so that she replies back in a whisper.

To enable whispered response mode simply open the settings section on your Alexa app. You will find it under "Alexa Voice Responses" under your Alexa Account .

Make life More Entertaining with Alexa

New Music Service – TIDAL

The global music streaming platform TIDAL has partnered with Amazon and soon its services will be available on all Echo devices.

Left-Right Stereo Pairing

Now you can connect two of your Echo dots for a stereo sound using the left -right stereo pairing feature.

Amazon Music New Release Notifications

Now it will be possible to ask Alexa to follow your favorite artist and get notifications every time a new album or track of your favorite artist is released. You can get notifications for these on your Echo device or within the Amazon Music mobile app.

Overlapping Groups

It is now possible to add a single echo device to different multi room music groups. This would mean you're your Echo in the kitchen can be part of the "Kitchen" group as well as the "Downstairs" group

Preferred Speaker Setup

Setting up a preferred speaker for playing music in your Alexa app would mean that you can give her a command to play music and she would stream it from your default speaker.

SECTION #2

MAKE THE BEST USE
OF ECHO DOT

CHAPTER 9
Music

Playing Music on Alexa is the favourite activity reported by Echo Dot owners. The all new Echo Dot enables hands free control of your music so you don't have to worry about changing a song manually. All you need to do is tell Alexa to play your favourite song or that playlist you want to listen to, and it will execute your command.

The best thing about playing music on Alexa is that one has the choice of using multiple free or subscription based music streaming services. So, if you love either **Pandora**, **Spotify** or **iTunes** you can integrate your music with Alexa and play it with a *single voice command*. All you will have to do is go to the settings section in you Alexa app and choose a default music service, once that is setup you can ask Alexa to play a song, play an album or play custom playlists. If you prefer to listen to your own music collection, you can upload your music files to Amazon Music.

Alexa is getting smarter with each update and caters to the customised preferences of users. The smart voice recognition system will enable the device to recognize the speaker and play the song that that person likes. With machine learning, Alexa is programmed to automatically play your favourite song based on the number of times it has been played.

Commands to Play Music

To play music, start by using some of these commands. It takes some time to get familiar with what kind of commands work well with Alexa.

Say the word **Alexa** followed by any of the following commands.

Playback Control

- *"Play"*
- *"Skip"*
- *"Skip back"*
- *"Pause"*
- *"Continue"*
- *"Next"*
- *"Previous"*
- *"Repeat"*
- *"Shuffle"*
- *"Loop"*

Volume Control

- *"Volume 4"*
- *"Softer"*
- *Turn it Up"*

Equalizer Commands to Change Bass, Midrange and Treble

- "Alexa, turn up the bass"
- "Alexa, increase the midrange"
- "Alexa, turn down the treble"

Amazon Music Setup with Alexa

Amazon Music Streaming Services

Amazon has 2 kinds of music streaming services that give you a wide range of artists and genres. It will keep a track of what you like listening to and will provide you similar suggestions. Not just this, but it can also respond to your requests really quickly. You can also buy music from the Amazon store using Alexa Shopping.

1. Amazon Prime Music – This one comes FREE with Amazon Prime Subscription and includes 2 Million songs. This service is integrated with Alexa so all you need to do is give Alexa a command and you can enjoy hands free listening.
2. Amazon Music Unlimited – If you want a wider variety of songs, this paid subscription will give you access to 50 Million songs. It comes with a 30-day Free trial and is $9.99/month at that.

When it comes to listening to music on Alexa the Amazon **Prime members** and **Amazon Unlimited Music Subscribers** can use a wide range of commands to make the best use of the huge music collection on Amazon.

Say the **Alexa** word followed by any of the following commands.

General Commands

- *"Play some music"*
- *"Play more like this"*
- *"Play what is trending"*

Specific Commands

- *"Play the song, [title]"*
- *"Play the album, [title]"*
- *"Play songs by Taylor Swift"*

Genre or Mood

- *"Play some angry hip hop music"*

- *"Play some Jazz music from 50s"*

Customised

- *"Listen to my evening playlist"*
- *"Shuffle my yoga playlist"*
- *"Play songs from last Sunday"*
- *"Add this song to my playlist"*
- *"Play rock music for a Party"*

Audible/Kindle Books

- *"Read audiobook, (title)"*
- *"Read the book, (title)"*
- *"Play the kindle book, (title)"*

Music Setup on 3rd party services

Alexa supports a number streaming services on Amazon devices

- Spotify Premium
- Pandora
- TuneIn
- iHeartRadio
- Spotify
- SiriusXM

Link Third Party Music Services to Alexa

This is pretty straight forward and uniform for all the music services. To link a third-party service to Alexa just follow these steps.

- In the Alexa app, go to Settings
- Inside Settings go to Music
- Inside the Music section select from among the listed music services
- You will need to sign in to your preferred music service account and then enable the link to Alexa. Then follow the

commands and the link will be enabled.

Select Music Service Preference

To select a preferred music streaming service please follow these steps:

- Open the Alexa App
- Go to menu and tap on Settings
- Inside settings tap on Music
- Inside music tap on Choose default music services

Then choose your preferred music service and you are done.

Alexa Commands for Third Party Music Service

To play a song using a third-party service you will need to mention the service name while giving command for the song/playlist selection.

- "Alexa, play James Brown radio on Pandora."
- "Alexa, play Country Music on Sirius XM."

Pairing Echo Dot with External Speakers

Pairing Echo Dot with your Mobile Device

You can connect your Echo Dot with a mobile device via Bluetooth and play music using an app on your mobile device. Pairing is easy, make your mobile device Discoverable and then use the following Alexa command.

- "Alexa, pair"

Once the device is paired with Alexa you can use your Echo Dot as a speaker and play music using your mobile.

Pair Echo Dot with Bluetooth Speakers (Audio Out)

The all new Echo Dot can be connected to Bluetooth enabled

speakers. Only one speaker can be connected at a time to the Echo Dot. To connect please follow these steps.

- Open the Alexa app
- Scroll down and Tap the Devices icon
- Choose your device from the collection
- Select Bluetooth Devices
- Select Pair a New Device
- Select your proffered speaker from among the list available and then just follow the instructions as described on screen

Here is a list of Bluetooth speakers that are compatible with Echo Dot and other Alexa devices https://www.amazon.com/b?node=14048078011

One can also Pair Echo Dot with External Speakers using an Audio Cable for Audio Out.

Multi-Room Music with Alexa

If you want to play music across multiple Echo devices and supported speakers then create a Multi-Room Music group. To create a Multi-Room Music group please follow these instructions.

- Open the Alexa App and tap on Devices
- On the Device page, tap the + sign on the top right-hand corner
- From among the selection, please tap Multi-Room Music Speakers
- Create a Name for the group
- Tap on the device name that you want to include
- Tap Create Group.

Alexa Command for Multi-Room Music Playback

- "Alexa, Play (music selection) on (group name)"

Stereo Pairing

If you have multiple Echo devices of the same model in your home you can pair them as Left and Right speakers for Stereo Sound. The speaker set can only play music. To create a speaker set please follow these steps.

- Place the two devices at least 1m apart.
- Open the Alexa app and tap on Devices
- On the Device page, tap the + sign on the top right-hand corner
- From among the selection, please tap Add Stereo Pair / Subwoofer
- Tap on Speaker Sets, and then follow the instructions

Alexa Skills for Music

There are plenty of Alexa skills for music lovers. Whether you want music streaming, radio or podcasts, a wide range of skills are available. Here are the bestseller Alexa Music Skills.

My Pod

This Alexa skill can be used to play popular podcasts all in one place. You can create Playlists from podcasts, text RSS feed, MP3, internet radio, audio books and more. You can also add subscription based podcasts to this your playlists.

Sleep and Relaxation Sounds

This skill helps you play white noise to sleep well or to work peacefully. It has more than 125 high quality sounds to choose from.

TED Talks

This skill brings all the fabulous TED talks to you.

Affirmation Pod

The world's leading podcast not at your command.

The Dave Ramsey Show

This is a great podcast for money management.

CHAPTER 10
Voice Calling and Messaging

Alexa's new Calling & Messaging feature lets you make calls between any two Echo compatible devices, an Alexa app or mobile or landline number in the US, Canada or Mexico. You can also send and receive messages between calls between any two Echo compatible devices or an Alexa app.

The message recipients get speech-to-text message readouts via the Alexa app for iOS and Android devices.

Pre-requisites

A valid Amazon account, an Echo device and a phone number

Setup

To setup voice calling, go to the App on your mobile and select the 💬 icon and then just follow the instructions. It is pretty straight forwards.

Start a call from Alexa App

- In the app tap the 💬 icon to open the screen for conversation.
- Next, on the upper right-hand corner tap the person-shaped icon and select someone you want to call.

- Tap on Call icon to initiate a call.

Alexa to Alexa calls

If someone calls, you can see a green light on Echo Dot with Alexa telling you the name of person calling. You can also enable a ringtone if you want. If you want to take the call, ask Alexa to **answer** or say **ignore** in case you don't want to talk. If there is another in-coming call when you are speaking to someone, this call can be received on another Echo device.

How to Start a call from an Echo Dot

- You can only make calls to people who have enabled the call feature in their app
- Ask Alexa to call XYZ and she will make the call.

Alexa does not support calls for the below type of numbers:

- Emergency services numbers (e.g. "911")
- Dial-by-letter numbers (e.g. "1-800-FLOWERS")
- Premium-rate numbers
- N-1-1 numbers / abbreviated dial codes

Send a Voice Message from an Echo Dot

- You can only message to people who have enabled the call feature in their app
- Ask Alexa to message XYZ and she will send the message.

How to Block Calls and Messages

- Each contact has the BLOCK option, just tap on in and that particular contact will be blocked.

CHAPTER 11
Alexa as an Intercom with Drop In

Drop In is an optional feature of Alexa that allows users to connect instantly with family and friends using their Echo devices as long as they have given the user the permission to do so. When you Drop In on an Echo device the light ring will pulsing green and the call will start automatically without the need to answer it.

You can use this feature as an intercom if you have multiple devices at home.

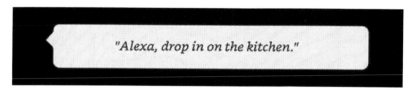

Set up Drop In

To use this amazing new feature what is required is an Echo Dot and a mobil with the Alexa app installed. It is worth noting that you can initiate a Drop in session with your Alexa app but it is not possible to receive a Drop in call on the app.

To use it as an intercom Drop In on a device in your home simply say, " Alexa , drop in on ......"

To Drop In on a device of a friend or family , first you need to get them to approve you to Drop In. Once that is taken care of you can say "Alexa , drop in on ....."You need to make sure the name is exactly the same as in your phone book.

Allow contacts to Drop in

Since the Drop in feature can be a breach of privacy , a device or app can only drop in if you have given permission to that specific contact to Drop in on you and they must do the same at their end for you to Drop in on their device.

To Enable contacts to Drop in

Open the Alexa App->Conversation tab -> Contact icon (top right)-> Select name -> Toggle the Drop in option

To remove contacts from Drop in

Open the Alexa App->Conversation tab -> Contact icon (top right)-> Select name -> Allow contact to Drop in anytime.

Manage Drop in Permissions

There are three levels of permission for the Drop in feature on any echo device

- On – All contacts that have been granted permission to drop in
- Only my household- Only household member devices can drop in
- Off – Drop in not available.

To temporarily stop Drop in

To stop Drop in on a specific device simply enable Do not Disturb

Alexa for Announcements

Announcements are like a one way intercom feature wherein you can ask Alexa to make an announcement to all the Alexa enabled devices on your account.

After you ask Alexa to make an announcement , a short chime is played on all the receiving compatible devices in the household, signalling the incoming announcement. After this the announcement will play in the announcer's voice .

If there is a specific device in your household who you do not want to receive the announcement , you can exclude it by turning on the Do Not Disturb feature. The device excluded can still send announcements though.

"Alexa, announce
dinner's ready."

CHAPTER 12
Alexa Smart Home

Wouldn't it be awfully convenient if you could have voice control over the lights, locks, and temperature in the house? Perhaps even things like the oven temperature and the cooking time? Echo Dot can handle smart lights, locks, can open and close garage doors, and control the temperature in the house as well.

Connect Echo Dot Smart Devices at HOME

To build your Smart Home, choose the Smart Devices you want to control from Amazon Echo Dot and connect them to your Alexa App directly or through a Smart Hub. Following is a list of devices you can choose from.

Devices Directly Controlled by Alexa

Following are few of the Smart Devices that can be directly controlled by Alexa via Wifi. (For a comprehensive list please refer to Appendix A1)

Lighting and Fans

- LIFX Wifi Smart LED Light Bulbs
- Haiku Wifi Ceiling Fans

Switches and Outlets

- Belkin WeMo: Light Switch, Switch (Smart Plug) and Insight Switch
- TP-Link: Smart Plug and Smart Plug with Energy Monitoring
- D-Link Wifi Smart Plugs

Thermostats

- Nest Learning Thermostat
- Ecobee3 Smarter Wifi Thermostat
- Sensi Wifi Programmable Thermostat

Locks

- Garageio
- Danalock

Car Control

- Automatic

How to Connect Smart Devices to Alexa

To connect these devices to your Amazon Echo Dot, please follow these simple instructions.

- Make an account for your Smart Device on its native app.
- Connect your Smart Device account to Amazon account.
- Use voice commands or the Alexa App to control the Smart Device.

Devices that need a Hub/Bridge to be controlled by Alexa

Lightning

- Philips Hue Series via Philips Hue Bridge/Starter Kit
- Cree Connected LED via Samsung Smart Things Hub or Wink Hub
- GE Link Bulb via Wink Hub
- Osram Lightify Smart Bulb via Wink Hub
- TPC Connected Smart Bulbs via Samsung SmartThings Hub or Wink Hub

Outlets, Dimmers and Switches

- iHome Smart Plug via Wink Hub
- Samsung SmartThings Outlet via Samsung SmartThings Hub
- GE Z-Wave Switches, Dimmers and Outlets via Samsung SmartThings Hub
- Leviton Switches, Dimmers and Outlets via Samsung SmartThings Hub or Wink Hub

Thermostats

- Honeywell Lyric/Total Connect Comfort Thermostats via Samsung SmartThings Hub
- Keen Home Smart Vents via Samsung SmartThings Hub

Why do we need Smart Home Hubs

Smart Hubs are necessary because a lot of Smart Devices in the market lack the radios required to enable direct communication with Echo Dot.

Alexa can control lots of smart home devices, but most of the integrations require a smart home hub that acts as a link between Amazon Echo Dot and the particular device. Amazon Echo Plus has an integrated Smart Hub, so if you are planning to use a lot of smart home devices, you can consider Echo Plus instead of Echo Dot.

Here is a list of prominent Smart Home Hubs you can buy today to and control your Smart Home Devices:

- Samsung SmartThings Hub
- Wink Hub
- Insteon Hub
- Philips Hue bridge/Starter Kit
- Caseta Wireless Smart Bridge
- Alarm.com Hub
- Vivint Hub
- Nexia Home Intelligence Bridge
- Universal Devices ISY Hubs
- HomeSeer Home Controllers
- Simple Control Simple Hub
- Almond Smart Home Wifi Routers

Control Your Smart Devices using Amazon Echo Dot

Basic Voice Commands

The following list of commands works really well with Alexa and have been tested.

ON Commands

- "Alexa, turn on <Device Name>"
- "Alexa, start <Device Name>"
- "Alexa, unlock <Device Name>"
- "Alexa, open <Device Name>"
- "Alexa, boot up <Device Name>"
- "Alexa, run <Device Name>"
- "Alexa, arm <Device Name>"

OFF Commands

- "Alexa, turn off <Device Name>"

- "Alexa, stop running <Device Name> (also very tricky)"
- "Alexa, lock <Device Name>"
- "Alexa, close <Device Name>"
- "Alexa, shutdown <Device Name>"
- "Alexa, shut <Device Name>"
- "Alexa, disarm <Device Name>"

DIM Commands

- "Alexa, brighten <Device Name> to <Position>"
- "Alexa, dim <Device Name> to <Position>"
- "Alexa, raise <Device Name> to <Position>"
- "Alexa, lower <Device Name> to <Position>"
- "Alexa, set <Device Name> to <Position>"
- "Alexa, turn up <Device Name> to <Position>"
- "Alexa, turn down <Device Name> to <Position>"

Advanced Voice Commands to Control your Smart Devices

- "Alexa, turn off/on the bedroom light"
- "Alexa, brighten/dim the kitchen light"
- "Alexa, lower/raise kitchen thermostat by 15 degrees"
- "Alexa, set kitchen thermostat to 74 degrees"

Grouping the Lights Together

Suppose after working in the attic you are tired and getting ready for bed, you want to switch off the lights. Not only those on the top floor, but also those in the porch and the hallway. Group them together and switch them all out by one voice command.

Amazon Echo Dot will work with any smart connected device linked to your home Wi-Fi network. But Amazon offers support only for a few lights and switches, the rest need to be controlled through a Smart Hub as mentioned earlier. These are BR30 down lights, Hue H19 traditional bulbs, Light and Bloom Strips, and Lux white bulbs. If you plan to use switches go with WeMo. The range includes LightSwitch, Insight Switch, and Switch.

Use Wink to group your lights and control your bulbs. You must connect it to Echo Dot. You can use this with GE Link bulbs if you so desire. You can even do more things such as opening blinds other than just open and close doors or switch lights on and off with the Wink App. Name each of the bulbs and give this group one name.

To Group the Lights

- Go to Settings inside the Alexa App.
- Here you must find Connected Home.
- Add Wink. It will find Connected Devices.
- Now, you can add your Group.

Once you do this, just command Alexa.

- "Alexa, turn on hall lights"

In this way, you can schedule a program to turn off the lights or use a single voice command such as, "Alexa, turn off all the lights" just before you go to bed.

CHAPTER 13
Echo Dot in the Kitchen

Alexa is good with controlling smart devices but she is also extremely useful when it comes to helping out in the kitchen by taking hands free commands. She can

- Help create and maintain grocery list
- Convert popular units used in the kitchen
- Step by step walk-through of a recipe
- Timer for food and preparation time
- Make your morning coffee
- Manage larger appliances in the kitchen

Create and Maintain grocery list

Now creating to do and shopping list will be a breeze with simply telling Alexa what you want to add and mention which list it needs to be added to.

For example, if you tell her "Alexa, add milk." As milk is a noun, she will understand that this is an item you want added to your shopping list. You can also tell her "Alexa, please add eggs to my shopping list".

- Alexa, add cheese to my Grocery List.

- Alexa, add eggs to my shopping list.
- Alexa, can you please add an item to my grocery list.
- Alexa, please add "visit grocery store" to the to-do list.

Convert Units

Imagine you are making preparations for a dinner for 6 and you just found a recipe that serves 4, Alexa can help you convert the recipe for 6 easily. Alexa also can convert units, which is a handy function when you are busy cooking and your hands are covered in four or meat. Alexa can answer basic conversion questions without any skill enhancement.

- Alexa, convert 2 cups to milliliters.
- Alexa, convert this recipe for 4 people.
- Alexa, how many teaspoons are in 3 tablespoons?

Start a timer/ alarm

Just say Alexa please start a timer for 15 minutes. After 15 minutes, she will chime until you ask her to stop. Set multiple timers and she can manage them at ease. Also check with her how much time is left asking or cancel a timer that is no longer needed.

You can also start an alarm for either a specific time or one that is relative. For example you can say "Alexa, Please set an alarm for 5 a.m." or you can tell her "Alexa, Please set an alarm clock for 30 minutes from now "

- "Alexa, how much time is left on the pizza timer?"
- "Alexa, remind me to check the oven in 5 minutes."
- "Alexa, set a pizza timer for 20 minutes."
- "Alexa, cancel the pizza timer."

Calorie count

Besides using Alexa for recipes you can also use it to track calories. Although it does not know all of the complex and unique foods that exist, it does know the basics. Alexa can provide all the available nutritional information it has.

- "Alexa, ask calorie counter to log food apple."
- "Alexa, ask calorie counter how many calories I've had today."
- "Alexa, ask calorie counter to delete my last food."
- "Alexa, ask food tracker how many calories are in 2 eggs and 3 slices of bacon?"
- "Alexa, ask food tracker how many carbs are in 3 ounces of pasta?"

Allrecipes

Get access to 60,000 plus of America's most loved recipes from Allrecipes.com. No need anymore to type, tap, swipe or squint to get the best recipes your family would enjoy. Just as Alexa and get the dinner ready in a breeze.

The Allrecipes Skill gives you the convenience of hands-free access to recipes be it for everyday dinners or dinner for family and friends. Alexa can help you quickly find recipes that meet your requirements - be it preferred cooking method, available cooking time, type of dish you would like to make or ingredients you have on hand. Alexa can help save recipes to Allrecipes Favorites and retrieve recipes later as needed. Ask Alexa to send the recipe to your phone, so you can quickly make a trip to the store for the ingredients. Want to give the recipe a new twist, Alexa can share what variations other cooks have made by sharing reviews with you.

You will need to provide her with your phone number (if you want recipes sent to your phone) and Allrecipes login information (if you want to retrieve or add recipes to favorites.

- Alexa, Open Allrecipes. (Opens the Allrecipes Skill)
- Alexa, ask Allrecipes what can I make with bacon, chicken and cheddar cheese?
- Alexa, Ask Allrecipes to find me the recipe for World's Best Pizza.
- Alexa, ask Allrecipes for a slow cooker recipe for pulled pork.
- Alexa, Ask Allrecipes to find me a chocolate chip cookie recipe from my Favorites.
- Alexa, ask Allrecipes for the recipe of the day?"
- Alexa, add this recipe to my Favorites.
- Alexa, tell me the reviews for this recipe.
- Alexa, send the recipe to my phone.
- Alexa, what ingredients are needed for this recipe?
- Alexa, open All Recipes and find me a chicken recipe that takes less than 45 minutes.
- Alexa, Ask All Recipes the next step.
- Alexa, send the recipe to my phone.

Control large appliances

Wouldn't it be nice if you could get out of bed and simply tell Alexa to make your coffee? You can! Simply utilize a smart switch and IFTTT programming. Simply remember your trigger phrase in the morning and you are good to go.

You can also control things like your dishwasher, oven or even your slow cooker with your Alexa enabled device.

Generate recipe ideas

Aside from the All Recipes skill, there are a number of skills that allow for the finding of recipes using your Amazon Echo or Amazon Echo These skills include:

Recipe Finder by Ingredient

- Alexa, ask Recipe Finder by Ingredient what I can make with chicken and corn
- Alexa, ask Recipe Finder by Ingredient what kind of sandwich can I

make with cheddar cheese

- Alexa, ask Recipe Finder by Ingredient to find me a recipe with eggs, condensed milk, and pumpkin.
- Alexa, ask Recipe Finder by Ingredient what can I make with chicken with mushrooms?

Trending Recipes & Food

- Alexa, can you get the latest recipe from Trending Recipes?
- Alexa, can I have the fifth recipe from Trending Recipes?
- Alexa, can you give me the most recent recipe in Trending Recipes?

Best Recipes

- Alexa, ask best recipes what's for dinner
- Alexa, open Best Recipes

Step by Step walk through for recipes

- Alexa, show me a slow cooker recipe from Allrecipes.
- Alexa, find me a pie recipe.
- Alexa, search for Chef John's Pumpkin Pie.
- Alexa, reviews.
- Alexa, how much time does the recipe take?
- Alexa, what is the recipe of the day?
- Alexa, recipe details.
- Alexa, find me a pumpkin pie recipe.
- Alexa, find me the Perfect Pumpkin Pie recipe

CHAPTER 14
Shopping On Amazon Echo Dot

It is not just about making shopping lists; Echo Dot can also be made use of for placing orders. Not just place orders, it can also help you in looking for alternatives. It can also remember your shopping lists; this feature comes in really handy if you want to reorder something.

If you want to order any supplies for office, you will need to make a list of all the things that you will need to get done. However, with the help of the Echo Dot, you can get it to place the order for the supplies that you require from the Amazon website or app. Then you will need to simply wait for your order to get delivered. You can make changes to or edit an existing order as well. If there are any common orders, then you can get Echo to repeat the same order.

Setup Voice Purchasing

You can buy digital and physical products from Amazon with your Alexa device using the 1-click payment method. You need a US/UK billing address and a payment method and Prime Membership (only for Physical Products) to enable voice transactions. Physical products order is also eligible for free returns.

When you register your Alexa device, Voice Purchasing is on by default.

You can use voice commands to carry out the following activities with your Echo Dot

- **Purchase** a Prime-eligible Item
- **Reorder** an Item
- **Add** an Item to your Amazon cart
- **Track** the Status of a Recently Shipped Item
- **Cancel** an order immediately after ordering it.

To Enable/Disable Voice Purchasing, activate an optional 4-digit confirmation code and check your payment method and billing address

- Open the Alexa App
- Tap Settings
- Voice Purchasing

Now you can access all the purchase settings, to make any required changes.

A few Categories in the physical products are **NOT ELIGIBLE** for voice purchasing.

- Apparel
- Prime Pantry
- Shoes
- Watches
- Prime Now
- Jewellery
- Amazon Fresh
- Add-On items

Now that you are all set for Voice Purchasing!

These are few commands you can use to make your first purchase on Echo Dot.

Alexa Shopping Commands

- *"Alexa, order (item name)"*
- *"Alexa, reorder (item name)"*
- *"Alexa, add (item name) to my cart"*
- *"Alexa, track my order "*
- *"Alexa, where is my stuff?"*
- *"Alexa, cancel my order"*

Buy Music using Echo

To shop for a song or an album use the following commands

- *"Alexa, Shop for the song [song name]"*
- *"Alexa, Shop for the album [album name]"*
- *"Alexa, Shop for the album [artist name]"*

Purchases are stored for free in your music library; they don't count against the storage limits, and are available for playback/download on any device that supports Amazon Music.

Manage your Shopping/To Do List

- Tap the main menu on your Alexa App
- Select Shopping & To-do Lists

You can add, remove or edit items on the list in the App itself or by using the voice commands. You can export these lists to Evernote, Gmail, Todoist or iOS Reminders by using IFTTT recipes.

CHAPTER 15
Alexa For Kids

Room filling sound with crisp vocals and dynamic bass response

Bedtime timer

To help children adjust to a good bedtime routine it is important for them to understand and accept the fact that bedtime is approaching. Instead of you holding the timer and playing the bad mama or bad dad, you can ask Alexa to set a timer for you.

Read your little one a bedtime story

Try getting Alexa to help in the bedtime routine while you are busy brushing your teeth or getting ready for bed yourself.

- She can connect to your Audible.com account and will read them stories available in your account.
- Alexa can use the skill - "Short Bedtime Story" to tell a personalized story to your children. She can tell a story to them personalized for them, with their name mentioned at various points. You can also customize and disable stories you do not want your children to hear and create new ones tailored to your family.

For example - When you ask Alexa to start narrating a story

She will start narrating a story like..."Once upon a time there was a magical wizard named Henry who came upon a little frog with blond hair. Henry asked the frog..."

- o Alexa, tell Bedtime Story to Allie
- o Alexa, launch Bedtime Story
- o Alexa, ask Bedtime Story to Configure

Play a few lullabies

Create a bedtime Lullaby playlist online so that Alexa can play it whenever you ask her to. What a great way to end a bedtime routine with a song each night!

Dim the lights

If you have the right light bulbs and dimmer switches in your child's room / nursery, you can just Ask Alexa to dim the lights once the bedtime routine nears an end.

White noise machine

Alexa can play your child white noise, although this does mean you will need to leave the device in the child's room / nursery and that may not be practical for your family.

Free Time on Alexa

Kid Routine

Parents can use a set of pre-defined Alexa routine templates to create their own custom-made routines for the younger members of the family. One can set After School, Good night and Good morning routines which can include personalized messages, white noise timers, light control, music control to name a few .

For example when Alexa is told, "Good night, Alexa" by the child or one of the parents, she would rely with a custom goodnight message, would turn on the night lamp , turn off the day lights and start white noise or smart sleep sounds based on the routine set up .

Kid Podcasts

With Free Time Unlimited, Kids enjoy Audible books, TV shows, games and music apps. Amazon has now introduced kid friendly podcasts including *Story Pirates* from Gimlet Media, and *Ear Snacks* from Andrew and Polly to the list of entertainment options available for kids .The podcast give access to educational as well as age appropriate news and stories to the children

Kid Activity Skills

Amazon is revamping its offerings in the Kid Activity Skill category by adding skills like Animal Workout, Train Like an Avenger, Star Wars Missions, Oregon Trail. This fun content helps families get enjoy together and use their imagination and entertain themselves.

CHAPTER 16
Alexa with IFTTT

IFTTT interface provides the easiest way to link various apps and functions with Alexa.

There are plenty of IFTTT recipes that you can use with Echo Dot to automate your life and carry out repeatable tasks to save time and effort. But first you need to connect your Amazon account with IFTTT.

- Go to IFTTT and setup an account if you don't have one
- Go to channels home page and select Amazon Alexa channel
- This will prompt you to enter your Amazon account info to sign in
- Once your sign in you can access all the existing recipes for Alexa
- Choose from among 800+ recipes and add them to your account

Smart Home Recipes in IFTTT

Temperature Control with Nest Thermometer

You choose a phrase and the temperature you want. Then, you say,

- "Alexa, set [phrase]"

And your room temperature is set according to your wish.

For doing this, first, go to the IFTTT and connect to the respective Nest channel.

- Open the Amazon Alexa Channel with your smartphone or computer.
- To do this, click on the three horizontal lines on the top left corner.
- Scroll down and choose Smart Home option.
- You come to the Device Links tab.
- Under this select Nest and click Continue.
- Log in with the Nest id and password.
- Now, you see Discover Devices.
- If Nest is on the local Wi-Fi network, Alexa will discover it.

Automate your Life with SIGNUL Beacon channel

It is an amazingly unique way of creating a bridge between your physical and digital world just by detecting the presence or absence of your smartphone.

Define your zone entry and exit events to Signul Beacon to help automate mundane tasks. The Channel will use your physical context to streamline your digital world.

Here are things you can do once this you fix up this channel.

- Upon reaching your desk, you are logged into a spread sheet
- Slack is informed when you arrived for work
- At bedtime, mute phone
- When you leave work, turn on Nest thermostat

To execute these hacks, connect to Signul Beacon Channel on your IFTTT account and start using it.

House lights go on at sunset

Set your lights to go off at sunrise and on at sunset by the use of WeMo switches. You can control one or a group of lights and since they do not require batteries as they are Wifi controlled, they can operate forever. You can use any brand of light, fluorescent, halogen, LED, incandescent, and fans with the WeMo switch. The program works well even if you experience a power outage. However, you cannot replace three-way switches.

Download the WeMo app from Google Play or iOS for your Smart phone. You can turn on WeMo or turn it off. But first, you have to connect the Wink Relay Channel and the WeMo Switch Channel on IFTTT. While we are here, you should know that Wink Relay channel fits well with WeMo switches, Android SMS, Tesco, Sensibo, Yo and EVE for Tesla.

Turn Hue Lamps Red or Green

Magic begins when you change the ambiance with just a single command. Alexa will turn your Philips Hue Lamp Green, Red or turn them off when you want. But, connect the Philips Hue Channel and your IFTTT Workflow Channel first.

Adding Devices

If you haven't done so already, here are devices you can add to your smart home. You will find all these under WeMo and devices in IFTTT

WeMo Devices

- Crockpot: You can add two different commands: one to cook slow and the other to turn it off. This helps you control your crockpot.

- Maker: With this you can turn on, turn off and let the appliance run for a while. You must set the appropriate command as "Alexa, turn on (off) the sprinklers" or "Alexa, set pool pump for 20."
- Coffeemaker: This helps you brew coffee.
- Switch: Plug any device you wish to control into the WeMo Switch such as turn on a lamp in the morning at 7 AM or turn on lights when I arrive home.

Sonos

- "Alexa, play the front room Sonos"

Quirky Aros

- "Alexa, turn on Aros"
- "Alexa, turn off Aros"
- "Alexa, set Aros to 80"

Music Recipes in IFTTT

IFTTT Integration for Music

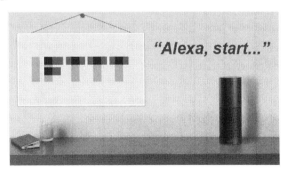

Set up the smart Hi-Fi system in every room. Connect to Musaic to improve the sound quality of your music. If you connect the lights to Music, you will get party lights when the music begins. Also, you can wake up with music streaming and night-lights fade.

And don't miss out on the Deezer channel. With Deezer, you can take your music with you to every place you go. Use Add new tracks to make a fast addition of the tracks you want to Deezer.

- Sync your favorite songs to SoundCloud
- Add artist
- List favorite songs on Evernote
- Listen to favorites from SoundCloud on Deezer
- Add favorite to Google spread sheet

Connect to music with Musixmatch

Connect your favorite songs to Musixmatch.

Spotify Playlist

For those who have an Apple account, you can create a Spotify playlist from your Apple Music Playlist. Connect to Spotify Channel and Workflow Channel to execute this.

SoundCloud

This app SoundCloud has many recipes that give music a new meaning. Share your SoundCloud tracks to Facebook; sync them to your Spotify collection; Use Genius to follow the songs you like on SoundCloud or share new songs to Tumblr.

Work recipes in IFTTT

How to Note events with precise time and people on your calendar

First, go with your mobile or computer browser and connect the Google channel. To improve on this functionality, use the Slack channel to connect this note with every member of your team or family. An alternate way to do this is to go to Amazon Alexa settings. Click on Calendar and pen in a new event.

How to Schedule for Repeated Tasks

Improve your schedule with the Google Calendar and your regular schedule. Do this daily or once every week to create more thinking space and organize your work schedule. For this, the Trello channel will not only serve as a reminder for these repeating tasks but also help you make plans.

How To Share your workflow with the iOS phone

Create a workflow and connect the Workflow Channel and Google Drive Channel. This now enables you to share a web page or text with Google Doc. If you use Slack, then you may send your message or web page. The two channels to connect are Slack Channel and Workflow Channel.

How To Set up DocSend Channel

Use this channel to keep track of the documents you send. Connect to various recipes and get informed when any person reads 100% of your document, post message to Slack channel whenever you have a new visit to a document, get an email of all the 100% document reads, remind me to follow up when someone reads 100% of my document (this could be your family member reading a family update) and much more. You can add this channel to these given here.

- If Channel: You can use the Get Notifications from the If Channel if someone visits and reads 100% of your document.
- FollowUp.cc: This helps our intrepid blogger or businessperson to keep 'with it'. You follow-up and see the reads. Connect first to start at this site.
- Slack: Post to the Slack Channel if you get a new visitor and if anyone reads 100% of your document.
- ORBneXt: In this, your Orb will flash when you have a visitor or anyone reads through the entire document.

- **Gmail**: This is the most popular internet device and you can connect DocSend channel to improve communications. You will get an email when you have a visitor.

How To Connect Fitbit through IFTTT

Go to this website and connect the two channels given there, the Fitbit channel and Google Calendar channel. Now, Alexa will remind you to go to sleep on time and adjust your sleep schedule according to the quality of sleep recorded the previous night. And you have your activity on a Google Spreadsheet.

SECTION #3

HAVE FUN WITH ALEXA

CHAPTER 17
Play Games with Echo Dot

Alexa is known for its smart-home, news, music and productivity skills but if you thought she was all work and no play then you are, mistaken. She is full of wit and jokes and has a great sense of humor. She is a good games master and capable of playing games and can make your dinner parties a hit. Be it interactive stories or new round of Jeopardy or a round of Bingo, Amazon's voice assistant can keep you entertained for hours. Below are listed some of the best trivia and games skills for Alexa.

The Magic Door

It is an interactive "choose your own adventure" game using Alexa. There are at present nine stories to choose from including saving monkeys on a tropical island, helping the princess find her crown, helping gnome find a key or exploring a witch's spooky mansion. The story unfolds based on the choices you make and Alexa describes the scene as you go along. The game is targeted towards younger ears and as each story is only 5 to 10 minutes long it is very effective if you are trying to get the kids quickly to bed.

To get started tell Alexa to enable The Magic Door

The Wayne Investigation

The Wayne Investigation is another choose your own adventure game for Alexa. You need to investigate the death of Thomas and Martha Wayne - Bruce Wayne's parents. The choices you make will decide the course of your investigation and affect your ability to solve the mystery. It is a great game for fans of the Dark Knight although it does contains some content that may not be suitable for all ages.

Start the game by asking Alexa to open The Wayne Investigation.

Earplay

Earplay are thriller stories with an interactive twist where you play the part of a secret agent in a radio drama. As is with other choose your own adventure games the choices you make determines how the story unfolds.

Blackjack

You can now play numerous rounds of Blackjack with Alexa with the skill- Beat The Dealer. You can ask Alexa to read the rules or ask her to give you basic game strategy. You can also ask her to "deal", and then "hit" or "stand" as you choose. She will tell you what the dealer chose and whether it busted or you won the game. The result is recorded whether you won or lost. You can at any time check with Alexa if you won more than you lost. As the games can go on forever remember to say "Alexa, stop" to interrupt and get on with the game.

To enable of a game of blackjack simply say the following commands,

"Alexa, start a game of blackjack" or "Alexa, open The Dealer."

Christmas Kindness

One of the most positive skill alexa has to offer is Christmas Kindness. She will give you a daily suggestion of how you can be kind during the holiday season. Start your day with by simply saying, "Alexa, Open Christmas Kindness" and she will provide you a random idea about how to integrate kindness into your daily life this holiday season.

CHAPTER 18
Alexa Easter Eggs

Though the future is far away, there is no reason for us to not use the future technology today. Alexa may need to cover many more milestones to achieve perfection but the state it made is good enough. After all, one can search and find Easter eggs that the bunny (Alexa) has hidden away.

Fun Phrases to Try Out with Echo Dot

Here is a list of fun phrases you can try out with Echo Dot. This list has been compiled from various sources on the net and is not an exhaustive list as Alexa development team keeps on publishing more phrases regularly.

- What is your favorite color?
- Do you have a boyfriend?
- Where do babies come from?
- Which comes first; chicken or egg?
- Do aliens exist?
- Where do you live?

- Do you want to build a snowman?
- What is love?
- Who won best actor Oscar in 1973?
- May the force be with you!
- Who let the dogs out?
- To be or not to be?
- Who loves ya baby?
- Who is the walrus?
- How tall are you?
- Where are you from?
- Do you want to fight?
- Do you want to play a game?
- I think you are funny?
- Is the cake a lie?
- Random fact
- Roll a dice
- Tell me a joke
- Mac or PC?
- Give me a hug
- Are you lying?
- How many angels can dance?
- I want the truth
- What's in the name?
- Knock knock
- What are you wearing?
- Rock paper scissors
- Party time
- Make me breakfast
- Where are my keys?
- Party on, Wayne
- Beam me up
- Make me sandwich
- How much does the earth weigh?
- Tea. Earl Grey. Hot.
- Who is your daddy?
- Is there Santa?

- Best Tablet
- When is the end of the world?
- Count by Ten
- Can you give me some Money? (Ask twice)
- Do you believe in ghosts?
- Do you believe in god?
- Do you believe in life after love?
- Do you know Siri?
- Do you like green eggs and ham?
- Do you really want to hurt me?
- Fire photon torpedoes
- Good night
- High five!
- Do you make bread?
- How many calories are in (name a food)?
- Live long and prosper
- Never gonna give you up
- One fish, two fish
- I'm home
- I've fallen and I can't get up
- I am your father
- Tell me a story
- Will you marry me?

Special Animal Sounds

Meantime, you can have loads of fun with special music and soundtracks. Amazon Prime members have access to this while non-members have to pay $0.89 for each track of animal sounds. The tracks themselves are interesting and you should look at the customer reviews of each one before you purchase them. You can get the best ones that way with ease. The collections include bird sounds (favorite with nature lovers and meditation freaks), animal sounds ("Alexa, what did the dog say this morning") and various mixes.

CHAPTER 19
Settings and Troubleshooting

Change the Wake Word

The default wake word is ALEXA.

You can choose from among four of the following wake words.

- Alexa
- Echo
- Amazon
- Computer

To change is wake word on your mobile or computer

- Open Alexa app.
- Go to the control panel.
- Select **Settings** for the Echo device for which you want to change the 'wake word'.
- You will see Wake Word listed for each device.
- Click on this and select the new 'wake word'.
- Now click **Save.**
- This change is possible only on Echo and Echo Dot.

Working with the Remote

Remote does not come in the Echo box but can be purchased separately.

The remote has a microphone, a talk button, and Playback controls. To talk, you press the talk button and talk. The playback button helps you to Play or Pause, Increase or Decrease the Volume, and switch to Next or Previous. The advantage when you use the remote is that you need not 'wake' up Alexa with the 'wake word'. This proves invaluable for those who have more than one Echo units and do not want to disturb the one on the top floor when 'talking' the one in your living room.

Reset to Factory Default

If you are having trouble with your Echo Dot you can restart your device to see if it resolves your problem.

If this does not solve your problem then you can follow the steps mentioned to reset your Echo Dot.

To **Reset** your Echo Dot:

There's a tiny buttonhole that is present near the bottom of the device, besides the plug. You will need to insert a pin and press this button for resetting the device. The light ring will turn orange and then turn blue. This means that your Echo Dot has been reset. You can turn it off and turn it on again till the light ring on top turns white and cyan.

Is Alexa Spying On You?

No. Alexa is not spying on you. Alexa only pays attention to you when it hears the designated wake word. Rest of the time, although technically it is on all the time and always on a look out for the wake word from you, it does not record your voice.

But if you are still worried that Alexa will hear and record any private conversations, you can push MUTE button and Echo Dot will not hear or follow anything you say.

How to Ensure Alexa Stops Listening

Press the MUTE button on top of the Echo Dot. The top LED ring will turn red when the mute is ON. You can unmute by pressing the same button again.

There have been zero cases of people using Echo Dot for illegal activities till date. However, to take further precaution and prevent any kind of monkey business from your Echo Dot device ensure that you:

- Do not position the Amazon Echo Dot near any window.
- Do not position the Echo Dot close to any speakerphone or answering machine.
- Mute your Amazon Echo Dot device when away from home.

However you need to know that Echo Dot uses machine learning to study your voice pattern from past recordings and improve its response to your questions. You can delete these voice recordings, but in doing so you may degrade your user experience with Echo Dot.

Troubleshooting

Sometimes the Echo Dot does not listen to your voice or hangs carry out the following steps to get it back in action.

- Ensure that your device in not on MUTE. Check the LED ring in not RED. If it is RED, press the MUTE button again and start speaking.
- Ensure that Echo Dot is not receiving a software update.
- Unplug the device and leave it off for 60 seconds and then plug it back again. It should mostly come back online by performing this action.
- If it still does not respond, leave it unplugged for a few hours and then plug it back again.
- Still Struggling? Try to reset your Echo Dot You will need to setup the device again so try to use this step sparingly. However, in most cases this does the trick.
- If the problem still persists, try to contact Amazon Customer Support.

Can't connect to the Bluetooth?

If you aren't able to connect your mobile device to the Amazon Echo

Dot using Bluetooth the here are a few steps that you can follow.

Ensure that the device you are trying to connect is within 30 feet of the Amazon Echo.

The Bluetooth connection needs to be turned on.

Your mobile device needs to be paired with the Amazon Echo Dot and if it isn't paired you will need to say "Alexa pair".

From the Bluetooth settings on your mobile device select the options Amazon list so that it can connect to the device.

If you are still having trouble, then follow the following steps.

- Open the Alexa app and go to the Settings in it. Select the name of your Amazon Echo Dot from the options. This will clear all the devices that are currently paired.
- Unplug the power cord from the Amazon Echo Dot and then plug it back in after 30 seconds.
- Now retreat your mobile device again. Once the device is on you can turn the Bluetooth on from the settings menu.
- Say "(your wake word), pair". On your mobile device will need to open your setting menu and choose the option Echo-####
- You need to select the name of your Amazon Echo Dot from your mobile device. Amazon Echo Dot will respond with "connected with Bluetooth "if the connection was successful.

Echo Dot keeps disconnecting from my network?

This seems to be a common problem that a lot of Echo Dot users have been facing. Here are some things that you can try for solving this problem.

- You should reset your router: On your router, there should be a reset button, but the location of this can vary depending on the manufacturer and the model. If this does not work then

- Try rebooting your router: You will need to turn the router off and wait for 30 seconds before it back on. When you do this the Wifi services on the other devices will be interrupted. So, before you reboot the router you should probably ensure that no one is doing anything critical on his or her devices. So that they can save their work before the Wifi is turned off. If there's no improvement then move on to the next step.

- Reboot the router and let the Wifi be connected to only the Echo Dot and no other device: Yes, this indeed is a troublesome process. But it has proven to be effective. The Echo connects better when it is the first priority in the order of the Wifi connections. So, this means that you will need to disconnect all the other devices that are connected to the Wifi before you turn the Wifi on again. By doing this you will be able to ensure that the Echo Dot is going to get connected first. And once your Echo Dot is connected you can reconnect all the other devices.

- Get a backup power supply for your router: if you happen to reside in an area where there are brownouts or disruption in the electrical supply for a brief period of time, then you should consider getting a backup power supply for the router you are using. Even if the disruption was for a few seconds your entire Internet connection can be down. So, you will have to reset the main box. Still no luck, then try this

- Upgrade your router: if you are tech savvy, then you can fiddle with the settings of your router and try and optimize the connection to your Echo Dot. But it can be the case of having too many devices that are connected to the same router. Routers have a capacity to accommodate only a certain number of devices. Any additional device will cause excessive load on the router and it won't get connected. So, upgrading your router might be a good idea.

Echo isn't able to hear you clearly?

It can so happen that your Echo Dot might not be able to hear you clearly. Most often it is the problem with the location of the Echo. When the Echo is near any wall, the audio tends to bounce back. This causes a literal echo that can confuse the speech recognition ability of the Echo Dot. It could also be due to any interference from other electronic devices and this could cause the inability of the Echo Dot to recognize your commands. So, all you need to do is find a sweet spot for your Echo Dot so that it works better. The Echo Dot mobile app helps you not only record what the Echo Dot heard you say but it also gives you an option to let you decide whether or not Echo Dot heard you right. You can make use of this feature of deciding the best location for your Echo Dot.

Look around the room and think of a possible list of places where you can place the Echo, but the location chosen needs to be near an electrical outlet. You should also avoid all those places that have an uneven surface where the Echo Dot might get knocked over and also avoid those places where are any vents nearby including other sources of heat or cold. For each of the possible locations for the Echo Dot, you need to follow the instructions give here. You will need to plug the Echo Dot in the location that you desire and wait for it to say that it's ready. The place that you usually stand or sit at, say this to the Echo Dot "(wake word), your new location". For instance, you can say "Alexa: you are now on the coffee table".

If you are in the habit of interacting with your Echo Dot from different locations, try each of these in turn and add the different locations to the statement you are making. Like "Alexa: you are on the coffee table and I am in the foyer." Notice whether or not the light blue highlight that's present on the LED ring at the top the Echo Dot is oriented towards your current location. This light is supposed to provide the indication of where the Echo Dot thinks you are. At times you will also get default error responses like, "I can't find the answer to the question I have heard", you needn't worry about this. Remember that you aren't trying to get a valid response from the Echo Dot. You can check the mobile Echo app to see whether or not the Echo Dot heard you properly.

When you are done with the above things then you should review the results of the placement test. By now you should have a good idea of the possible locations where the Echo Dot can hear you and these places are the typical places suited for your Echo Dot. So, all you need to do is move your Echo Dot to the new location you have decided on and you can enjoy much better conversations with Alexa.

Cannot discover a connected home device?

If Alexa isn't able to discover a smart home device then here are the steps that you can follow. The first thing that you will need to try would be:

- The home device you are trying to connect should be compatible with Alexa.
- You will need to link your third-party account for devices that are connected to a hub, like Wink for instance.
- Check whether or not the device is set up properly in the companion app of the device. You can contact the manufacturer or visit their website if you aren't able to set up the device.
- Through the manufacturer's companion app you can update the software of your smart home device. These updates will help in improving the Wifi connection of the device.
- For discovering a smart home device on your Echo Dot, you will need to connect Alexa to the same Wifi network. For updating your Wifi in the Alexa app, you will need to go to the settings, select the name of the device and click the option update Wifi.
- Personal Wifi networks are best suitable for Alexa and other smart home devices. Also, the Wifi devices at school or work might not allow unrecognized devices to connect to them.

How to delete your Voice Recordings

- Open your Alexa app
- Tap Settings
- Tap History.
- Here, you will see a list of requests you have made since setting up your Echo.
- Tap a recording and delete it

CONCLUSION

I hope this book has helped you make Amazon Echo Dot an important part of your life and enabled you to organize your life seamlessly with Alexa at your command.

Continue on with your wonderful journey with the power of Amazon Echo Dot. Hope your doubts are removed and your life has eased. Since this is only the beginning, you will find more comfort and happiness with Alexa as you get more fluent with the device and the interface.

Do You Want To Stay Updated With Alexa?

As discussed in the beginning of this book, please find the URL for the signup to our FREE weekly Alexa Newsletter. Each week we will send you NEW ways to use your Amazon Echo at Home, Work And Play.

http://bit.ly/alexa_echo

The Amazon Echo and Alexa Enabled Devices are still in their infancy. In fact you are one of the EARLY ADOPTORS of this technology. The smart assistant industry is changing so fast with new devices, apps and skills being released almost every other day that it is almost impossible to STAY FRESH.

Staying in the know about new developments in the Smart Assistive Industry is what we are here for. Do not worry, we hate spam as much as you do and your details will be safe with us. Please go to http://bit.ly/alexa_echo to signup.

Did you like this Book?

Let everyone know by posting a review on Amazon. Just click here and it will take you directly to the review page.

If you have any specific questions that you could not find an answer for in this book or elsewhere we would be pleased to help you. Do write to us, our email address is majesticnotebooks@gmail.com

OTHER BOOKS YOU MAY LIKE

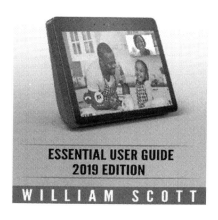

Made in the USA
San Bernardino, CA
06 March 2019